FELIX MENDELSSO

G000075101

DIE HEBRIDEN

THE HEBRIDES

Overture for Orchestra
Op. 26

Ernst Eulenburg Ltd

London · Mainz · New York · Paris · Tokyo · Zürich

MENDELSSOHN

Overture, The Hebrides

At Fort William, early on Friday 7 August 1829, Mendelssohn and his friend Carl Klingemann caught one of the new paddle-steamers that were running between Inverness and Glasgow through the recently-opened Caledonian Canal, and it took them forty miles down Loch Linnhe to Oban, through some of the loveliest scenery in Europe. Mendelssohn was twenty at the time. From Oban Harbour he walked a mile up the coast and began a pencil sketch of a mediaeval ruin called Dunollie Castle; he was able to include Loch Linnhe and the distant mountains of Mull in the background. He did not have time to finish the sketch because they had another steamer to catch. That evening they embarked for Iona on the *Ben Lomond* (70 tons) which took them from Oban as far as Tobermory, Mull's only harbour; there they spent the night 'in a respectable private house'. Before going to bed Mendelssohn wrote home, heading his letter 'On one of the Hebrides'. The letter contained a famous sentence and twenty bars of music: 'In order to make you understand how extra-ordinarily the Hebrides have affected me, I have written down the following which came into my mind' (see page VII below).

This was the first summer that steamer trips to Staffa and Iona had been advertized, and Mendelssohn had planned such a trip before leaving Edinburgh, but it cannot have been Staffa and Iona that so 'extraordin-arily affected' him because he did not set eyes on them until the following day. Those evocative bars were inspired by islands and sea between Fort William and Oban or (more probably) between Oban and Tobermory.

However on 8 August the *Ben Lomond* sailed on into the open Atlantic, and the passengers were put ashore for an hour or so on both Staffa and Iona. Iona was inhabited and probably provided refreshment, but Staffa is uninhabited, tiny and very rocky. Its one attraction is Fingal's Cave with its remarkable basalt pillars like organ pipes. Fingal was the Celtic hero of the translations from Ossian that Macpherson had published around 1760—translations that were still admired on the continent, though suspected in Britain of being largely Macpherson's invention. Whether they were or not, there is no evidence to link Fingal with this cave. Then, as now, landing on Staffa was dangerous except in calm weather, and because the passengers did land (Klingemann mentions a stout old lady determined to go ashore in spite of the scrambling) it must then have been fairly calm. Yet Klingemann wrote, with all the smugness of the man who has not himself been affected: 'The Atlantic stretched its tentacles around us with increasing roughness, knocking us all over the place . . . The ladies went down like flies and so indeed did the gentlemen; I only wish my travelling companion had not been among them, but he's on better terms with the sea as a composer than as an individual or a stomach.' Instead of circumnavigating Mull as it would today, the steamer returned from Iona past Staffa to Tobermory. Mendelssohn may have been in good enough shape to appreciate Staffa in the afternoon, but he can then have seen it only from a distance.

The point is of some interest. He called the first draft of his overture *Die einsame Insel* ('The Lonely Island') and on publication the full score was headed *Fingals Höhle,* and for these reasons it has often been assumed that Staffa was the lonely island and the chief inspirer of the music. This is possible but unlikely. In Mendelssohn's published letters there is no mention of Staffa; all he seems to have remembered of 8 August was 'the most fearful sickness'. Furthermore he is said to have disliked the catch-penny title his publishers foisted on him, and the probable reason is that Fingal's Cave did *not* inspire the music, Staffa was *not* the lonely island; as has been shown above, the main theme had come to him elsewhere. Mull itself looks extremely lonely from the sea, as well as splendidly beautiful. If this seems too large an island, there are much smaller ones in the vicinity; for instance Calvé, just outside Tobermory harbour. The passengers had expected to be back in Oban late on the Saturday, but the steamer was far behind schedule and the captain anchored for the night in Tobermory Harbour. Very early on the Sunday morning the *Ben Lomond* sailed for Oban, and Mendelssohn and Klingemann immediately set off for Glasgow.

Mendelssohn did not compose his best works as fluently as has sometimes been supposed. He took nearly three years over his *Hebrides* overture, writing out two quite different versions of it; each of the MSS contains many alterations. He finished the first version in Rome on 16 December 1830, and it is headed *Die Hebriden*, but someone took a copy of this MS before Mendelssohn had made most of the alterations, and this copy is headed *Die einsame Insel*. More than a year later, on 21 January 1832, Mendelssohn wrote to his sister Fanny and told her that he still considered the overture unfinished. 'The loud D major section in the middle is very stupid, and the so-called development smacks more of counterpoint than of oil and seagulls and dead fish; and it should be just the opposite.' With a London concert in view he was already working on his second version of the overture, and this had its first performance on 14 May at a Philharmonic Concert with the composer conducting. In the light of this performance he made a few further adjustments, and the score was finally completed in London on 20 June 1832, as he noted on the MS. In the first edition of his Dictionary Sir George Grove mentioned that the published score and parts did not always agree, for instance in bars 7 and 87. No doubt this was because the published parts had been taken from those used at the first performance and took no account of the later adjustments.

Only a very rough indication can be given here of the many differences between the 1830 version, *A*, and the final one, *B*. The figures on the left are bar numbers in *B*.

1–5   Fag II originally doubled the Contrabasso, but in the final version of *A* these notes were crossed out.

33–46   These bars replaced 10 quite different bars in *A;* the latter included the wind tune in 45–6 but without the semiquaver accompaniment.

70–98   These bars replaced quite different and less interesting music beginning in the more predictable key of G minor.

132–148   New. *A* had no triplets and continued to develop, rather too conscientiously, the theme in bar 1.

170–174   These 5 bars replaced 12 bars in *A*.

189–190   Between these bars Mendelssohn cut four bars of recapitulation (more or less the same as bars 19–22).

232–243   These bars replaced 21 bars in *A*.

In addition *A* had clarinets in C, no *sf* in bar 23, a less interesting rhythm for the wind in 98–109, no double bar or *Animato* at 217, and the clarinet phrases in 264–5 an octave higher on the flute. It will have been noticed that since scribbling the opening bars in Scotland Mendelssohn had halved their note values.

Mendelssohn's surprising wish that his music should express the realities as well as the beauties of the Hebrides makes one wonder if he ever managed to make it do so to his own satisfaction. The calm sea of his second subject and the storm music are obvious to every listener, but where is the oil? Perhaps bars 149ff represent the chugging of the little paddle-steamer. There is evidence that Mendelssohn was very interested in the new steamers, and indeed in machinery of all kinds, but it must be added that this passage was already present in *A*.

The facts about the two versions of the overture can be summarized as follows:

A Die Hebriden. MS finished in Rome 29 December 1830; never printed, but this version was performed at the Crystal Palace, London, 14 October 1871. MS published photographically in Basle in 1948 (the British Museum copy is Hirsch M 281). While it was owned by Moscheles, Gounod added a minim D in bar 3, bottom stave, and wrote underneath that he thought it had been left out by mistake. Before many of the alterations were made, someone made a copy of this score; it is called *Die einsame Insel*, carries no date, and is now deposited in the Bodleian Library, Oxford.

B Die Hebriden. MS dated London 20 June 1832; a very free revision of *A*; substantially the version performed in London on 14 May 1832. It was published in full score in 1835 by Breitkopf and Härtel under the title *Fingals Höhle;* the parts had appeared the previous year under the much-to-be-preferred title *Die Hebriden*.

Information about Mendelssohn's travels is taken or deduced from the letters he and Klingemann wrote, and from Mendelssohn's diaries and dated pencil sketches, now in the Bodleian Library, Oxford. Information about steamer trips in 1829 is taken from *West Highland Steamers* by Duckworth and Langyard (3rd ed., Glasgow 1967), and verbally from Anthony Browning of Kelvingrove Museum, Glasgow.

Roger Fiske, 1974.

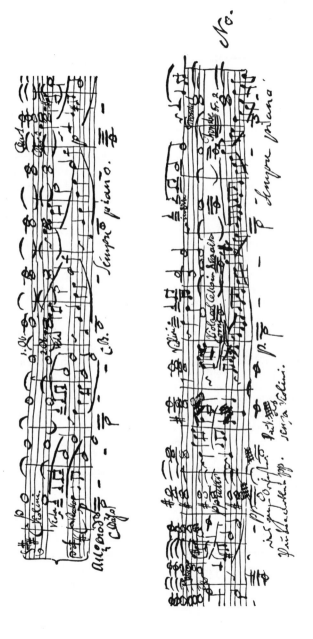

MENDELSSOHN

Ouvertüre, Die Hebriden

Am Freitag den 7. August 1829 begab sich Mendelssohn mit seinem Freund Carl Klingemann in der Frühe auf einen der neuen Raddampfer, die zwischen Inverness und Glasgow durch den damals erst kürzlich eröffneten Caledoniankanal verkehrten. Die vierzig Meilen lange Reise ging Loch Linnhe hinunter bis nach Oban, durch eine der landschaftlich schönsten Gegenden Europas. Mendelssohn war damals zwanzig Jahre alt. Vom Hafen in Oban ging er eine Meile an der Küste entlang bis zu einer mittelalterlichen Ruine, die Dunollie Castle hiess, und von der er begann, eine Bleistiftskizze zu machen. Es gelang ihm, Loch Linnhe und die fernen Berge von Mull im Hintergrund einzubeziehen. Doch hatte er nicht die Zeit, die Skizze zu vollenden, weil er und sein Freund noch einen anderen Dampfer erreichen mussten. Am selben Abend schifften sie sich auf dem *Ben Lomond* (70 Tonnen) ein, der sie von Oban bis nach Tobermory, dem einzigen Hafen auf der Insel Mull, trug. Dort verbrachten sie die Nacht ,in einem respektablen Privathaus'. Bevor er sich zu Bett legte, schrieb Mendelssohn nach Hause und gab seinem Brief die Anschrift ,Auf einer Hebride'. Dieser Brief enthielt einen berühmt gewordenen Satz und zwanzig Takte Musik: ,Um Euch zu verdeutlichen, wie seltsam mir auf den Hebriden zumute geworden ist, fiel mir eben folgendes bei' (vgl. S. VII).

Es war der erste Sommer, in dem Dampferausflüge nach Staffa und Iona angekündigt wurden, und Mendelssohn hatte einen solchen Ausflug schon geplant, bevor er Edinburgh verliess; doch können es nicht Staffa und Iona gewesen sein, bei denen es ihm so ,seltsam zumute' geworden ist, denn er hat diese Inseln erst am folgenden Tag zu Gesicht bekommen. Jene stimmungsvollen Takte wurden durch die Inseln und die See zwischen Fort William und Oban, oder (und das ist wahrscheinlicher) zwischen Oban und Tobermory, inspiriert.

Jedoch am 8. August dampfte der *Ben Lomond* weiter und auf den offenen atlantischen Ozean hinaus, und die Passagiere wurden für ungefähr eine Stunde auf Staffa sowohl wie auf Iona ausgesetzt. Iona war bewohnt, und Erfrischungen waren daher vermutlich erhältlich, aber Staffa ist unbewohnt, sehr klein und sehr felsig. Die einzige Sehenswürdigkeit auf dieser Insel ist die Fingalshöhle mit ihren merkwürdigen Basaltpfeilern, bie wie Orgelpfeifen aussehen. Fingal war der keltische Held der Ossian-Übersetzungen, die Macpherson um 1760 herausgegeben hatte. Diese Übersetzungen wurden immer noch auf dem europäischen Kontinent bewundert, während man Macpherson in Grossbritannien verdächtigte, sie selbst erfunden zu haben. Wie dem auch sei, für die Verbindung von Fingal mit dieser Höhle, gibt es überhaupt keine Unterlagen. Damals, wie heute, war es gefährlich, in Staffa anzulegen, ausser bei ruhiger See, und da die Passagiere tatsächlich an Land gingen (Klingemann erwähnt eine beleibte alte Dame, die entschlossen war, sich trotz der Kletterei auf die Insel zu begeben), muss es wirklich ziemlich still gewesen sein. Allerdings schrieb Klingemann auch, mit all der Blasiertheit von einem, der nicht betroffen war: ‚... die Atlantische (See) – das reckte seine tausend Fühlfäden immer ungeschlachter und quirlte immer mehr – ... und überhaupt fielen die Ladies um wie die Fliegen, und ein und der andere Gentleman tat's ihnen nach; ich wollte, mein Reisepechbruder wäre nicht unter ihnen gewesen, aber er verträgt sich mit dem Meere besser als Künstler, denn als Mensch oder als Magen.' Anstatt um die Insel Mull herumzufahren, wie das heute geschieht, fuhr der Dampfer von Iona, an Staffa vorbei, zurück nach Tobermory. Es ist möglich, dass sich Mendelssohn am Nachmittag gut genug gefühlt hat, um die Ansicht von Staffa würdigen zu können, doch kann er die Insel dann nur in der Ferne gesehen haben.

Das ist nicht ohne Bedeutung. Er gab dem ersten Entwurf seiner Ouvertüre den Titel *Die einsame Insel*, und als die Partitur veröffentlicht wurde, erschien sie unter dem Namen *Fingals Höhle*. Aus diesen Gründen hat man häufig angenommen, dass Staffa die einsame Insel war, und dass sie in der Hauptsache die Musik inspiriert hat. Das wäre möglich, ist aber unwahrscheinlich. In Mendelssohns veröffentlichten Briefen wird Staffa nicht erwähnt. Von all dem, was sich am 8. August zugetragen hat, scheint er nur die ‚grässlichste Seekrankheit' in der Erinnerung behalten zu haben. Überdies heisst es, dass er den Reklame machenden Titel, den ihm seine Verleger angehängt hatten, missbilligt hat, und der wahrscheinliche Grund dafür ist, dass die Fingalshöhle die Musik *nicht* inspiriert hat. Wie weiter oben dargelegt wurde, war Staffa *nicht* die einsame Insel, und das Hauptthema ist ihm woanders in den Sinn gekommen. Von der See gesehen, sieht Mull selbst höchst einsam und ausserdem herrlich und schön aus. Sollte man diese Insel als zu gross ansehen, so könnte es sich auch um viel kleinere ganz in der Nähe handeln, wie zum Beispiel um die

Insel Calvé, die gerade ausserhalb des Hafens von Tobermory liegt. Die Passagiere hatten erwartet, spät am Samstag abend wieder in Oban einzutreffen, aber der Dampfer hatte sich sehr verspätet, und der Kapitän liess das Schiff über Nacht im Hafen von Tobermory ankern. Am Sonntag früh dampfte der *Ben Lomond* ganz früh nach Oban, und Mendelssohn und Klingemann machten sich sofort auf den Weg nach Glasgow.

Mendelssohn hat seine besten Werke nicht so im Fluss komponiert, wie man es mitunter angenommen hat. Die Komposition der *Hebriden-Ouvertüre*, die er in zwei ganz verschiedenen Fassungen niedergeschrieben hat, beschäftigte ihn nahezu drei Jahre lang, und beide Manuskripte enthalten viele Änderungen. Er vollendete die erste Fassung am 16. Dezember 1830 in Rom und gab ihr den Titel *Die Hebriden*; aber irgend jemand verfertigte eine Abschrift dieses Manuskripts, ehe Mendelssohn den grössten Teil der Änderungen vorgenommen hatte, und diese Abschrift steht unter dem Titel *Die einsame Insel*. Über ein Jahr später, am 21. Januar 1832, schrieb Mendelssohn an seine Schwester Fanny und teilte ihr mit, dass er die Ouvertüre immer noch als unvollendet betrachtete. ‚Der Mittelsatz im *forte D dur* ist sehr dumm, und die ganze sogenannte Durchführung schmeckt mehr nach Contrapunkt, als nach Thran und Möven und Laberdan, und es sollte doch umgekehrt sein.' Für ein geplantes Konzert in London, hatte er sich schon mit der zweiten Fassung der Ouvertüre an die Arbeit gemacht, und diese Fassung wurde am 14. Mai erstmalig in einem der Philharmonischen Konzerte unter der Leitung des Komponisten aufgeführt. Diese Aufführung hatte zur Folge, dass er einige weitere Berichtigungen vornahm, und die Partitur wurde schliesslich am 20. Juni 1832 in London vollendet, wie das Datum im Manuskript besagt. In der ersten Ausgabe seines Musiklexikons erwähnte Sir George Grove, dass die veröffentlichte Partitur und die Stimmen nicht immer übereinstimmten, wie zum Beispiel in den Takten 7 und 87. Das kam zweifellos daher, dass die gedruckten Stimmen auf den Stimmen beruhten, die bei der ersten Aufführung benutzt worden waren, weshalb die später hinzugefügten Berichtigungen im Druck nicht berücksichtigt worden sind.

Von den vielen Unterschieden zwischen der Fassung *A* aus dem Jahre 1830, und der endgültigen Fassung *B*, können hier nur einige angedeutet werden. Die links stehenden Zahlen beziehen sich auf die Taktnummern in *B*.

1–5 Fag II spielte ursprünglich mit den Kontrabässen, aber in der endgültigen Fassung von *A* wurden diese Noten ausgestrichen.

33–46 Diese Takte stehen anstelle von 10 von ihnen völlig verschiedenen Takten in *A*, welche die Bläsermelodie der Takte 45–6 enthielten, aber nicht die Sechzehntel in der Begleitung.

70–98 Diese Takte stehen anstelle völlig verschiedener und weniger ansprechender Musik, die in der hier eher zu erwartenden Tonart G-Moll begann.

132–148 Neu. In *A* standen keine Triolen, und das Thema aus Takt 1 wurde, etwas zu gewissenhaft, weiter entwickelt.

179–174 Diese 5 Takte stehen anstelle von 12 Takten in *A*.

189–190 Zwischen diesen beiden Takten strich Mendelssohn vier Takte der Reprise (mehr oder weniger die gleichen Takte wie T. 19–22).

232–244 Diese Takte stehen anstelle von 21 Takten in *A*.

Ausserdem hatte *A* Klarinetten in C, kein *sf* in Takt 23, einen weniger lebendigen Rhythmus für die Bläser in 98–109, weder einen Doppelstrich noch die Bezeichnung *Animato* in 217, und die Phrasen für die Klarinetten in 264–5 standen eine Oktave höher für die Flöte. Es wird aufgefallen sein, dass Mendelssohn, seit dem Skizzieren der Anfangstakte in Schottland, die Notenwerte halbiert hat.

Mendelssohns überraschender Wunsch, die Musik solle die Realität sowohl wie die Schönheit der Hebriden ausdrücken, lässt die Frage aufkommen, ob er je mit dem was er in diesem Sinne erreicht hat, zufrieden gewesen ist. Die stille See seines zweiten Themas und die Sturmmusik sind für jeden Hörer deutlich genug, aber wo ist der Tran? Möglicherweise stellen die Takte 149ff. das Stampfen des kleinen Raddampfers dar. Es ist erwiesen, dass sich Mendelssohn lebhaft für die neuen Dampfer, und überhaupt für Maschinen aller Art, interessiert hat, doch muss hinzugefügt werden, dass diese Passage schon in *A* stand. Die wesentlichen Angaben über die beiden Fassungen der Ouvertüre lassen sich folgendermassen zusammenfassan:

A Die Hebriden. MS am 29. Dezember 1830 in Rom vollendet; nie gedruckt, aber diese Fassung wurde am 14. Oktober 1871 im Crystal Palace in London aufgeführt. MS photographisch 1948 in Basel veröffentlicht (das Exemplar im British Museum trägt die Bezeichnung Hirsch M 281). Zu der Zeit, als es sich im Besitz von Moscheles befand, fügte Gounod ein D (halbe Note) im dritten Takt des untersten

Liniensystems hinzu und schrieb darunter, er nehme an, dass diese Note versehentlich fortgelassen worden sei. Ehe noch viele der Berichtigungen eingetragen wurden, hat irgend jemand eine Abschrift dieser Partitur hergestellt. Sie trägt den Titel *Die einsame Insel*, aber kein Datum, und befindet sich zur Zeit in der Bodleian Library in Oxford.

B *Die Hebriden*. MS gibt Ort und Datum, London 20. Juni 1832, an; eine sehr freie Bearbeitung von *A*; in grossen Zügen die Fassung, die am 14. Mai 1832 in London aufgeführt wurde. Die Partitur erschien 1835 bei Breitkopf & Härtel mit dem Titel *Fingals Höhle*; die Stimmen waren schon im Jahr vorher unter dem Titel *Die Hebriden*, der dem anderen sehr vorzuziehen ist, erschienen.

Einzelheiten, die Mendelssohns Reisen betreffen, stammen aus den von ihm und Klingemann geschriebenen Briefen, sowie aus Mendelssohns Tagebüchern und datierten Bleistiftskizzen (die sich in der Bodleian Library in Oxford befinden), oder sind aus ihnen hergeleitet worden. Die Auskunft über Dampferausflüge im Jahre 1829 stammen aus der Veröffentlichung *West Highland Steamers*, Verleger Duckworth and Langyard (3. Ausgabe, Glasgow, 1967), sowie aus mündlichen Angaben von Anthony Browning vom Kelvingrove Museum in Glasgow.

Roger Fiske, 1974
Deutsche Übersetzung Stefan de Haan

Programatic overture, has a story.

It has scotish influences.

THE HEBRIDES

♩ ♫ ♩ ♩ = theme / motif

Overture

Ambiguous harmony – old rocks

Felix Mendelssohn-Bartholdy, Op. 26
1809 - 1847

A p

B mi *Sequence D*

no trombones

Cello links to both 1st + 2nd Subject

E. E. 3737

Ernst Eulenburg Ltd

Violins take up opening Cello in bar 8.

2

adds to rumble

rumbling of the deep in lower Strings

E.E.3757

4

E.E.3737

6

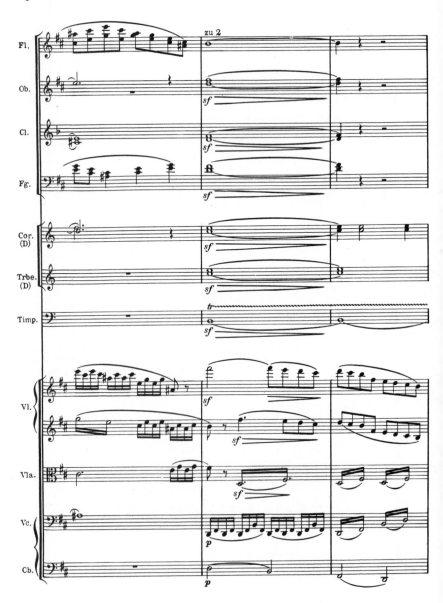

E.E. 3737

Handwritten annotations (student markings on the score):

Top margin: "Changed note lengths / Changed intervals based on ope[ning] / Bridge motif / so can / mo[..]"

Top right boxed: "y¹" and "x¹"

Left margin (vertical): "Tessitura - bring to conclusion."

Middle of page: "D₇D# resolving to C" — "I ∨ Bm"

Lower markings: "Bm" — "I ∨" — "repeated F# in sequence↑" — "C#↑ / inv" — "D# / inv" — "C#↑ / inv"

Bottom: "33-34-35-36-37-38, link to 1st subject"

Center bottom: "E. E. 3737"

Instrument labels: Fl., Ob., Cl., Fg., Cor. (D), Trbe. (D), Vla., Vc., Cb., Vl.

Rehearsal number: 30
Page number: 8

E. E. 3737

11

violins take
turn
copy
exact
by
28ve
4

^6_4Ic V^5_3 I

E. E. 3737

a new direction

E. E. 3737

E. E. 3737

19

E. E. 3737

fanfare dominates

22

E. E. 3737

alternating 1st subject with fanfare. continually modulating unrelated keys.

E. E. 3737

D

28

E. E. 3737

E. E. 3737

Most classical Sonata form movement recapitulation restablises home key.

36

200

2nd Subject - B major

tranquillo assai

quiet, tranquil
Sustained accompaniment.

Shorter

38

E.E.3737

turbulent
changing keys

not normal

Fugue like but contropuntal.
B minor

Fairly Significant
longer than Recap.
Just happens to fit
with program.

E.E.3737

237

Fl.
Ob.
Cl.
Fg.
Cor. (D)
Trbe. (D)
Timp.
Vl.
Vla.
Vc. e Cb.
240
Vl.
Vla.
con fuoco
Vc. e Cb.
con fuoco

246
Originaly in brass now in wood
Fl.
zu 2
f
Ob.
zu 2
f
Cl.
zu 2
f
Fg.
zu 2
f
Cor. (D)
Trbe. (D)
Timp.
Vl.
Vla.
Vc. e Cb.

E.E. 3737